MISSA BREVIS

FOR

FOUR VOICES

BY

PALESTRINA

EDITED AND ARRANGED FOR MODERN USE BY
HENRY WASHINGTON

───────────

Duration of performance 25 minutes

──────────

Chester Music
(A division of Music Sales Limited)
14/15 Berners Street, London W1T 3LJ

PREFACE

PALESTRINA wrote more than ninety masses. Among the few in general use *Missa brevis* ranks high in popularity. It may well have been a favourite from the time of its first publication in 1570, since the Third Book of Masses in which it was included was reprinted at intervals between the years 1590 and 1620. True, the same book contained such masterpieces of contrapuntal ingenuity as the five-part masses *Repleatur os meum* and *L'homme arme*, the appearance of which, according to Cametti, may have been Palestrina's reply to a charge that his work displayed more of fantasy than of learning. In our own day, at any rate, the popularity of *Missa brevis* is beyond question. This perhaps is due as much to its genial melody, ' modern ' tonality and suitable liturgical length, as to undoubted musical qualities of a profounder kind.

Several suggestions—none conclusive—have been put forward to explain the word *brevis* in the title of this mass. One is that it may be identical in meaning with *sine nomine*, a title commonly given to masses based on original themes as distinct from those based on themes borrowed from other compositions. This view conflicts with the findings of Ambros who has called attention to the resemblance of the themes of *Missa brevis* to those of an earlier work by Goudimel entitled *Audi filia*. Dr. Henry Coates points out, however, that at least one of Palestrina's motifs—that of the *Benedictus*—is not thus derived and that most of them can more convincingly be attributed to a Plainsong origin.

Haberl's explanation of *brevis* is different entirely. He refers it to the use of the *nota brevis* as the initial note of this mass. But against this should be set the fact that an initial *nota brevis* was a common feature of the style of the period and is found in other masses by Palestrina himself.

Perhaps, after all, *Missa brevis* means precisely what it says : a short mass ; for although it is by no means the shortest of all Palestrina's masses it is substantially shorter than some. It is one of a large number of comparable length—most for four voices—clearly intended for use *In Dominicis infra annum*, while those written on a more extended scale were reserved for the celebration of the major feasts of the Church.

One may observe an interesting disparity between the original publication of 1570 and the reprint of 1599. In the latter, issued five years after the composer's death, the Altus part of the *Hosanna* in the *Benedictus* has been revised by an unknown hand. Most modern editions, including those by Proske, Haberl and Rockstro, are taken from this reprint and carry the Altus variant.

The present edition restores the 1570 version as being more consistent with the style of the movement as a whole, in spite of the unusual dissonance treatment which the variant of 1599 was presumably designed to efface. The original was included—with an obvious misprint—in Alfieri's *Raccolta di musica sacra* ; in more recent times it has also been preferred by Casimiri.

One is tempted to speculate on the origin of the apparent licence. The absence of movement on the third beat (p. 24, bar 48) is not without precedent in Palestrina style, but in such a case the syncope on the second beat is normally consonant. Did the original printer mistake D for C ?

Certain practical features of the present edition require explanation. The music text is here set out unencumbered with arbitrary marks of expression. Thus, while the choirmaster is at liberty to insert such guides to performance as he thinks expedient, singers are spared the embarrassment of a live interpretation which conflicts with printed directions. At the same time the needs of inexperienced choirs have been met by incorporating in the *reductio partiturae* a suggested scheme of interpretation which may freely be modified—or totally ignored—in accordance with varying conditions of presentation.

It may here be mentioned that the Roman custom of introducing *ritenuti* at certain portions of the text, notably mention of the Holy Name, cannot always be observed without doing violence to the music. Often the composer has expressed the appropriate reverence by the use of longer note-values ; the choirmaster should then consider carefully whether conditions demand any underlining of this effect.

After much thought a system of regular barring has been decided upon, having regard to the fact that the training and equipment of the present-day choral singer bear little relation to those of his 16th-century counterpart. Experience has shown that, with average singers, any advantage to the rhythmic flow of irregularly-barred systems, or of the *Mensurstrich* (bar-lines placed metrically between the staves), is outweighed by difficulties of counting and place-finding.

The original note-values have been halved to conform to present-day acceptance of the crochet as the normal unit of time.

The sign ⸓ , a short vertical stroke placed above or below a note, is freely used throughout this edition with the twofold object of defending the verbal rhythm against the accentual power associated with the modern bar-line and of defining the true agogic rhythm where an original long note has been replaced by two tied notes of shorter duration. If singers familiar with the Solesmes rhythmic editions of the Chant should confuse this sign with the vertical *episema* no harm will result, though the sign is here used in a more restricted sense. On the other hand, the usual dynamic signs, bound up as they are with the idea of sudden stress, have been rejected as unsuitable for the purpose.

Missa brevis is written in the transposed Ionian mode. It is here reproduced in the original transposition, but may be performed a semitone or even a whole tone lower according to the vocal resources available.

The few original accidentals are printed in the usual place, *i.e.* to the left of the note affected. Other accidentals added by the editor in accordance with the theory of *musica ficta* appear in small type above the note and are confined for the most part to a naturalizing of B flat under the usual conditions.

The slur is used exclusively to denote an original ligature.

As to the underlaying of the verbal text, it should be noted that Palestrina treats the word *Kyrie* alternatively as of two syllables or of three. In this edition the syllable *rie* is to be pronounced " ree," the final *e* being elided.

No attempt has been made to distinguish the original arrangement of the words —often incomplete and at best merely approximate—from the solution of repetitions and other dispositions made by the present editor. In this he has been guided by the rules formulated in Palestrina's lifetime by Zarlino and Vicentino. The breathing requirements of average choristers have also been taken into account and it is intended that breathing points should be governed by the natural punctuation of the text.

It is not surprising to find that an occasional passage, by reason of a particular procession of note-values, appears to defy the strict application of the above-mentioned rules for underlaying the text. In such a case there is no alternative but to set down the least offensive of possible ' barbarisms.'

HENRY WASHINGTON.

THE ORATORY,
LONDON.
September, 1950.

MISSA BREVIS

KYRIE

PALESTRINA
Edited by
HENRY WASHINGTON

CH 08782

GLORIA IN EXCELSIS DEO

CREDO IN UNUM DEUM

SANCTUS

BENEDICTUS

AGNUS DEI I

AGNUS DEI II

The Chester Books of Motets

The first sixteen volumes of this expanding series are devoted to a wide range of sacred renaissance motets with Latin texts, and contain a mixture of well known and unfamiliar pieces, some of which are published here for the first time. All appear in completely new editions by Anthony G. Petti.

1. **The Italian School** *for 4 voices*
2. **The English School** *for 4 voices*
3. **The Spanish School** *for 4 voices*
4. **The German School** *for 4 voices*
5. **The Flemish School** *for 4 voices*
6. **Christmas and Advent Motets** *for 4 voices*
7. **Motets** *for 3 voices*
8. **The French School** *for 4 voices*
9. **The English School** *for 5 voices*
10. **The Italian and Spanish Schools** *for 5 voices*
11. **The Flemish and German Schools** *for 5 voices*
12. **Christmas and Advent Motets** *for 5 voices*
13. **The English School** *for 6 voices*
14. **The Italian and Spanish Schools** *for 6 voices*
15. **The Flemish and German Schools** *for 6 voices*
16. **Christmas and Advent Motets** *for 6 voices*

An index, complete with suggested seasonal use, covering the first sixteen books of the series, is printed in Book 16.

Chester Music
part of The Music Sales Group
14-15 Berners Street, London W1T 3LJ, UK.

Exclusive distributors: Music Sales Limited,
Newmarket Road, Bury St Edmunds,
Suffolk, IP33 3YB, UK.

CH08782

ISBN 978-0-7119-2897-8

9 780711 928978